Fun Crafts Christmas

Dear Christmas Crafters,

Almost as fun as opening presents on Christmas morning is pulling out and unwrapping our collection of Christmas decorations and ornaments from year to year. I love seeing the creations we dream up as the children grow and trends come and go.

I hope you enjoy making these crafts as much as we have. They range from super easy to a bit more advanced, with all the materials readily available at any craft store. Some you will be able to do as fun family projects, while others you will enjoy creating on your own, making your home and tree truly personalized and unique.

Merry Christmas!
Diana

You'll do a double-take to make sure this sweet wreath isn't made from miniature carnations. I made mine with a combination of solid-colored and printed tissue paper that coordinate with my specific holiday décor.

YOU WILL NEED

- 24 sheets of tissue paper
- Marker
- Flathead screwdriver
- 12-inch foam wreath/ring
- Glue
- Ribbon

Tissue Pom Wreath

1 Fold tissue: first in half lengthwise, and then in half again widthwise. Now fold accordion-style. Cut the folded tissue in half, and then fold each of those 2 pieces in half.

2 Draw cut lines with a marker, then with a screwdriver, make small slits over the lines on the top, front, and inside of the foam ring, approximately every 2 inches.

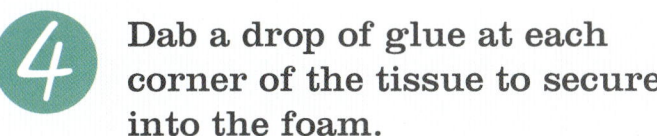

3 Insert folded edge of tissue "fan" into slit. (I use the screwdriver to push tissue into the foam.)

4 Dab a drop of glue at each corner of the tissue to secure into the foam.

5 Gently pull tissue paper open. (I find starting from the center and working out is easiest.) Tie ribbon around the ring to hang. Fluff tissue paper and hang.

My children love advent calendars. One holiday season I couldn't find one and my boys were so disappointed that I decided to make one. What I love about this one is that we get to use it year after year.

YOU WILL NEED

- ½ yard holiday fabric
- ½ yard canvas
- Straight pins
- Iron (optional if you would rather sew)
- Fabric glue
- Wooden dowel
- Ribbon
- Stencil
- Paint
- Scissors

1 Fold holiday fabric back about ¼ inch and iron to create a hem at the sides and bottom. Glue hem with fabric glue. Let dry. Fold top of fabric over to make a pocket for the dowel. TIP: Glue with dowel in place.

2 Cut canvas into 2" x 2" squares. Fold back the edges and iron.

3 Lay out 2" x 2" squares on large piece of fabric. Glue down the sides and bottom to create a pocket.

4 Stencil numbers 1 through 24 on the canvas pockets.

5 Tie ribbon onto or insert eyehooks into each end of the dowel and run ribbon through to hang.

6 Place a small treat or treasure in each pocket.

These lovely luminaries not only create a welcoming walkway for your guests, but also make a fantastic party favor for them to take home. These are inexpensive, quick, easy, AND they make a big impact!

YOU WILL NEED

- Bag of Epsom salt
- Large bowl and spoon
- Peppermint essential oil
- Mason/jelly jars
- LCD votive candles (1 per jar)
- Ribbon
- Gift tags and pen
- Holiday stamp, sprig of greenery, etc. (optional)

1 Pour salt into bowl. Add a few drops of peppermint oil. (You can always add more, but with pure essential oils, a little goes a long way.) Stir well.

2 Fill the jars about ¾ of the way full. Add a candle.

3 Tie ribbon around the top of the jar, and add a gift tag. (I like to write a small message on each one.) Add any other embellishments you like to personalize them.

Place luminaries along the path guests use to enter your home – and be sure to remind your friends to take one home when they leave!

Each December starts with testing last year's Christmas lights, resulting in a bucket of burned-out bulbs. But what to do with them? These reindeer are the solution, and are cute ornaments or gift toppers!

YOU WILL NEED

- Pipe cleaner (brown or tan)
- C9-style light bulbs recycled from old strands of lights
- Glue gun
- Hot glue sticks (or craft glue)
- Googly eyes
- Red bead or pom-pom
- Ribbon or ornament hanger

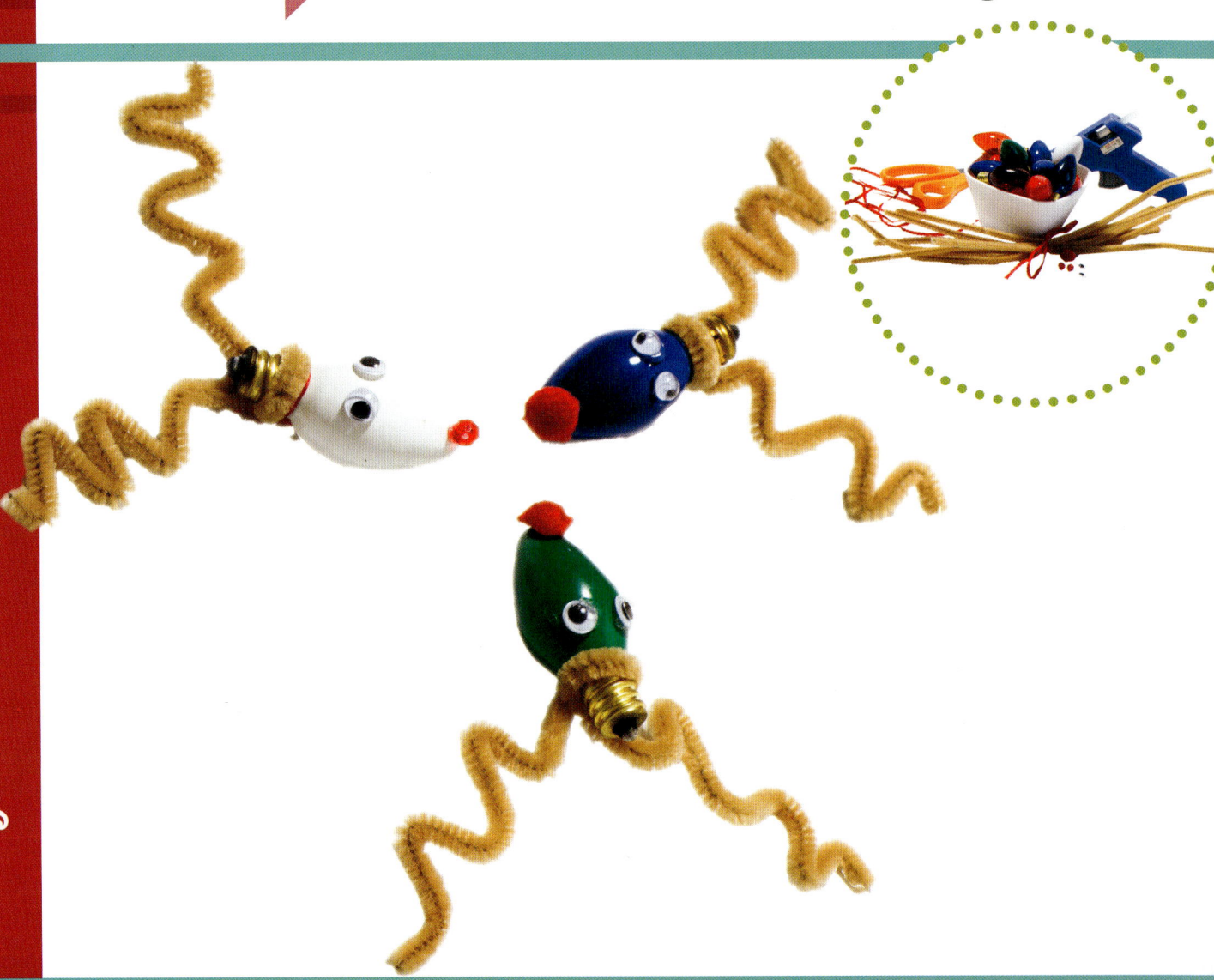

1 Wrap pipe cleaner once around the screw top of a bulb and twist to secure.

2 Bend the pipe cleaner to resemble antlers.

3 Dab 2 drops of glue to "face," then add googly eyes.

4 Dab a drop of glue at the bottom of the bulb, and add reindeer's red nose.

5 Attach an ornament hook or ribbon. Secure with a drop of glue.

When you see a pennant-style banner, don't you just know there's something to celebrate? I've made these for New Year's, birthdays, and, of course, Christmas. I love that they can be elegant, or fun and festive.

YOU WILL NEED

- Letters (You can use stickers, wooden craft letters, or stencil letters on another pattern of scrapbook paper.)
- Festive cardstock/scrapbook paper, 2 sheets more than letters you want to use. (I like to use paper that is printed on both sides.)
- Ruler
- Pencil
- Scissors (decorative-edge, if preferred)
- Hole punch
- Glue

Celebration Banner

1 Cut out or lay out the letters you wish to use.

2 Make a template for the banner by positioning the largest letter on the cardstock where you'd like it to be in the finished banner.

3 Lay your ruler to each side of the letter at an angle to create a triangle, and mark with a pencil. To make the template, fold the cardstock in half and cut along one marked side.

4 Unfold. Place the template on your cardstock and outline your banner to get the most triangles out of each sheet of paper. Cut out the desired number of triangles.

5 Using glue or tape, affix letters onto the triangles.

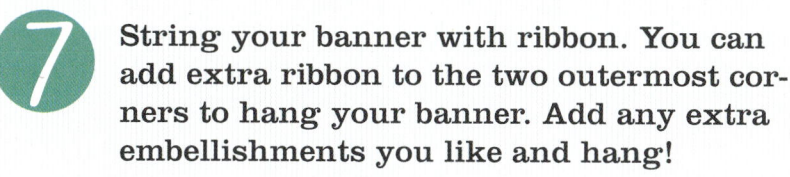

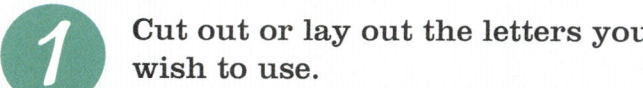

6 Punch holes or cut slits in the top corners of the triangles.

7 String your banner with ribbon. You can add extra ribbon to the two outermost corners to hang your banner. Add any extra embellishments you like and hang!

Every year I choose a few theme colors for holiday decorating. I use the same colors in ornaments, wrapping paper, and tablescapes. Here, I chose a solid-color balls, then added scrapbook rub-ons.

YOU WILL NEED

- Matte-finish Christmas balls
- Scrapbook rub-ons
- Ribbon
- Paint pens (optional)

Personalized Ornaments

1 Plan your layout of the rub-on. With a steady hand, rub the transfer onto the ornament with the implement provided.

2 You can continue personalizing by painting names or adding embellishments to your ornament.

3 Tie a coordinating ribbon onto the hanger, and hang on your tree, or give as a gift!

I put a bowl of paper strips in the middle of our dinner table, and each person writes three positive things about everyone, including themselves, and puts the strips back anonymously. We read them aloud before making our chain.

YOU WILL NEED

- Christmas scrapbook paper
- Pens
- Double-sided tape
- Bowl or tall glasses
- Decorative-edge scissors

1 Cut strips of paper approximately 1" x 8" long.

2 Write kind words about family and friends, or sentiments of gratitude from the year.

3 Loop a strip of paper into a circle and secure with double-sided tape. Continue with each strip, forming a chain.

4 Add to the chain each time anyone has something they want to show gratitude for.

You can hang from a doorway, your mantle, or your Christmas tree.

This project is super easy and a favorite for my tween girls. The beads pick up the lights from the tree and glisten like true icicles. They also make great present toppers!

YOU WILL NEED

- 20-gauge wire
- Needle-nose pliers
- Assorted beads
- Ribbon or hanger

1 Cut wire approximately 12 inches long.

2 Thread the first bead onto the wire, then, with needle-nose pliers, loop the wire over the bead. (This will make a stopper so the rest of the beads won't slip off.)

3 Continue threading beads in different patterns so all of your icicles will look different.

4 Leaving a bit of wire at the top (approximately ¾ inch), wrap the wire around the tube the beads came in to form your icicle. (Use a pencil if you don't have a tube.)

5 To finish, use pliers to form another loop at the top of the wire. Tie a ribbon on, or simply put on a hanger.

It's always fun to find an unexpected treasure. In these little, covered boxes, you can make winter scenes or hide a small treat. The outside of the box can be covered in whatever your imagination brings.

YOU WILL NEED

- Empty matchboxes
- Gold spray paint
- Wrapping paper, old Christmas cards, children's artwork, etc.
- Brads
- Ribbon for hanging
- Scissors
- Double-sided tape
- Glue
- Miniatures in holiday themes, or small treats such as candies or small tokens
- Glitter or trims (optional)

NICE

1 Spray inside of boxes with gold spray paint. Allow paint to dry.

2 Wrap outside of matchbox with giftwrap. (I find double-sided tape is the easiest to work with.) You could also use spray adhesive and glitter, or wrap the entire box with ribbon or trims.

3 Make small hole in top of inside box and push brad through to tie ribbon for hanger.

4 Decorate the inside of the larger boxes with miniatures to create holiday scenes. Fill smaller boxes with treats.

I laid these glass craft blocks out along with photos, paint pens, ribbon, stickers, and lights in my kitchen and let my family be creative. I was pleasantly surprised to see what great ideas they came up with.

YOU WILL NEED

- Stickers/Photos (optional)
- Chopstick
- Glass craft blocks
- String of lights
  (20-bulb strand, low watt)
- Ribbon
- Paint pens

1 If you are placing a photo or stickers inside the block, do this first.

2 Arrange lights inside the block. (Use a chopstick to spread out the lights.)

3 Tie ribbon around your block like a gift.

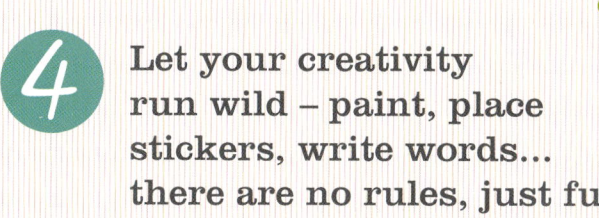

4 Let your creativity run wild – paint, place stickers, write words... there are no rules, just fun!

Growing up in Louisiana, "pokking" (like what a baby chick says: "pok, pok, pok") was a holiday tradition. Hang them on the tree and on New Year's Eve, let the "pokking" begin! Crack the egg over the head of an unsuspecting friend who will be showered in confetti!

YOU WILL NEED

- Eggs
- Confetti
- Tissue paper
- White glue
- Spray paint
- Spray adhesive
- Glitter
- Ribbon

Pok-Pok Eggs

1 Carefully crack the top off an egg and shake or blow out the contents. Rinse out and let dry.

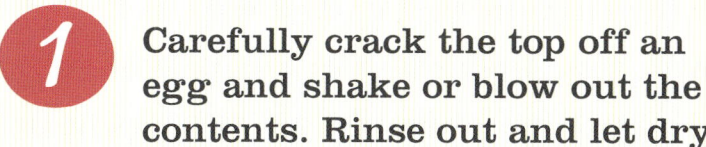

2 Fill with confetti and carefully cover the hole with tissue paper. Glue around edges. Let dry.

3 Spray paint egg desired color. Let dry.

4 Spray the egg with adhesive and roll in glitter.

5 Tie ribbon around the egg and hang from your tree.

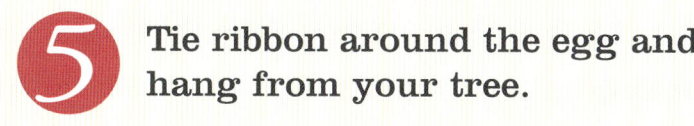

Holiday Crown

Who says party hats are just for birthdays? You never know when someone will need to be crowned "Queen of the Party," especially around the holidays! They're also great to have on hand for New Year's Eve.

YOU WILL NEED

- 2 pages of the same scrapbook paper
- Glue
- Pencil
- Scrap paper to draw template
- Scissors
- Hole punch
- Ribbon
- Assorted scrapbooking embellishments (stickers, flowers, beads, etc.)

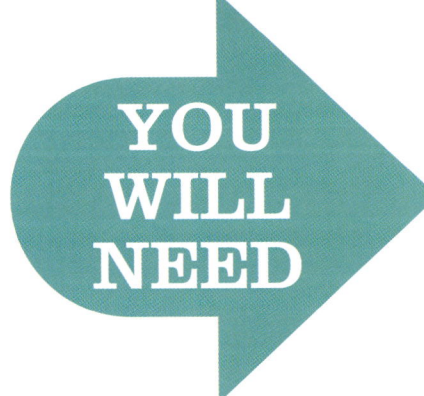

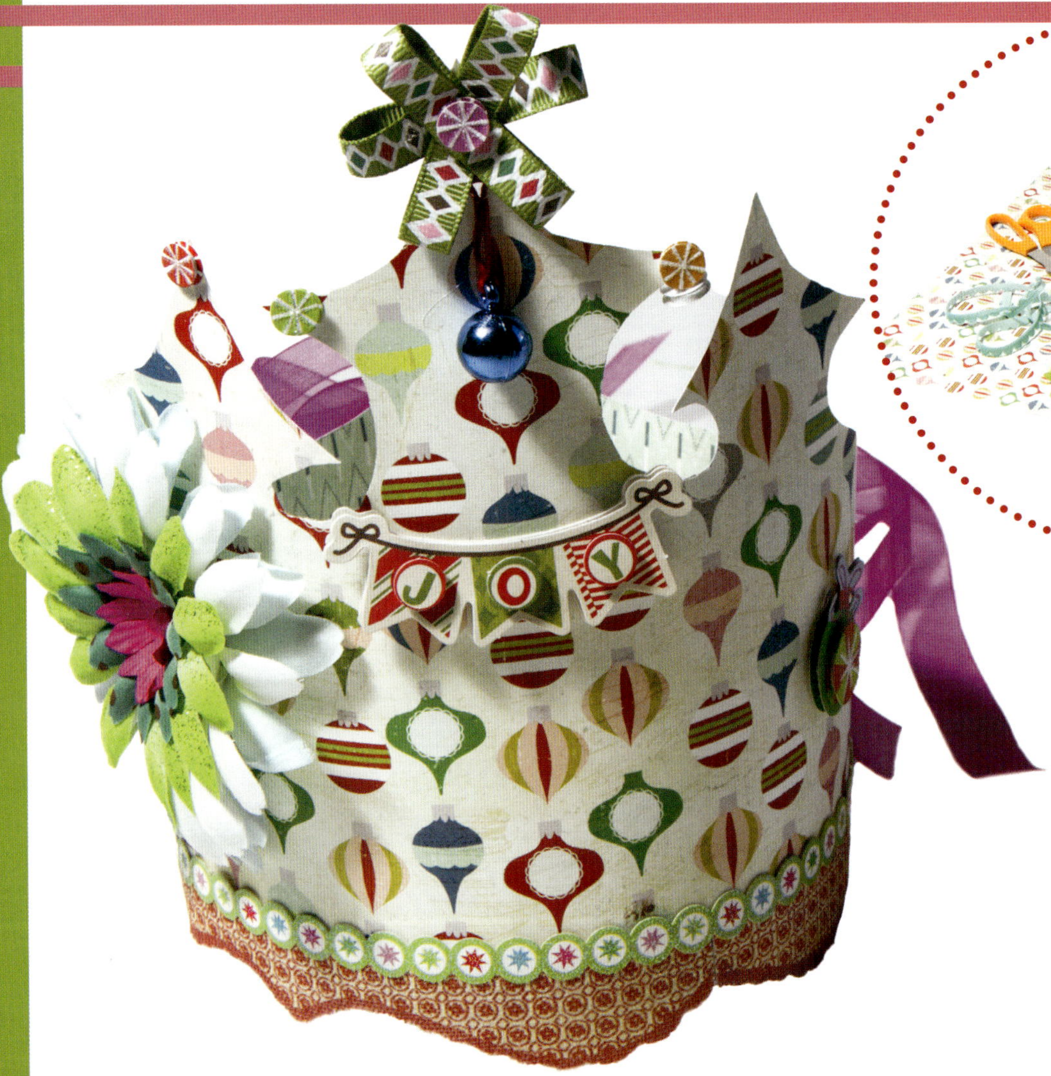

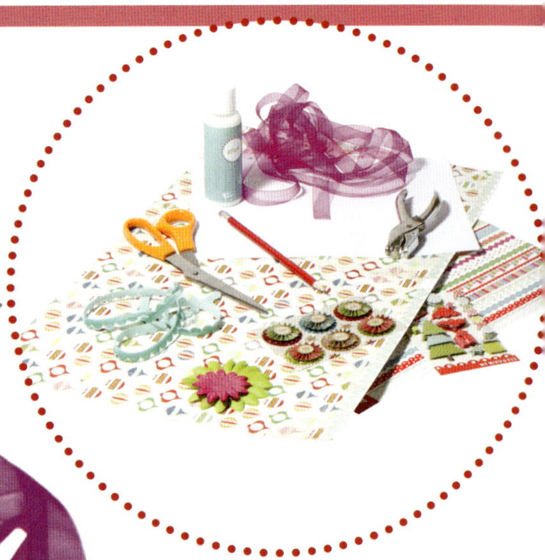

1. Glue 2 pages of scrapbook paper together, overlapping about ¼ inch to form one long page. Let dry.

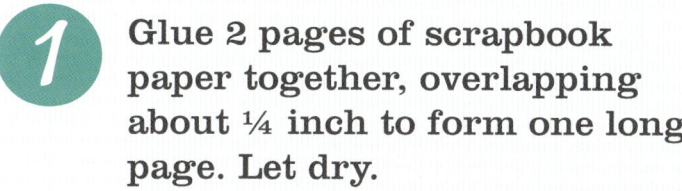

2. Sketch an outline of a crown on scrap paper, then cut out for your template. (I find allowing 1½ to 2½ inches in band height provides enough support for crown to hold its shape.)

3. Lay the template on the back side of the scrapbook paper. Trace and cut out.

4. Punch hole in each end of crown. Tie ribbon securely through hole punch, leaving ends long enough to tie in the back.

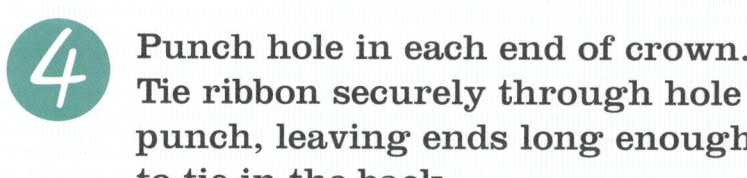

5. Embellish crown with an assortment of holiday stamps, stickers, flowers, or beads.

Pomander Balls

Pomander balls were made in the Victorian period to fragrance the home. My mother made these every year and passed the tradition down to my children. I always enjoy my boys bringing me a fresh batch.

YOU WILL NEED

- Ribbon
- Oranges (or any citrus fruit)
- Glue or long pins
- Toothpicks or meat thermometer
- Whole cloves

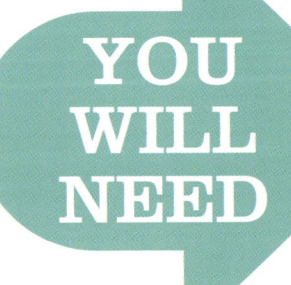

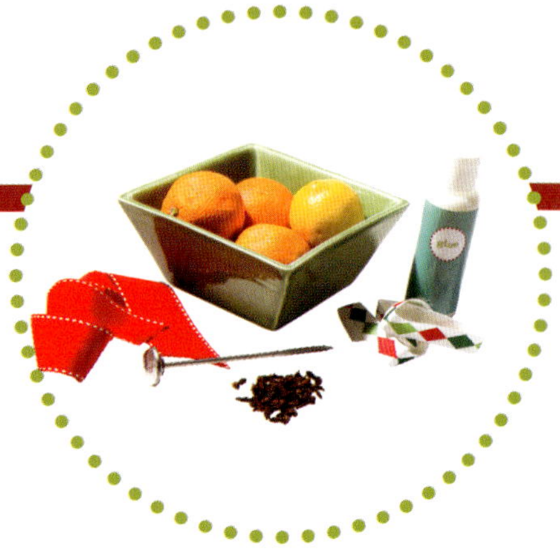

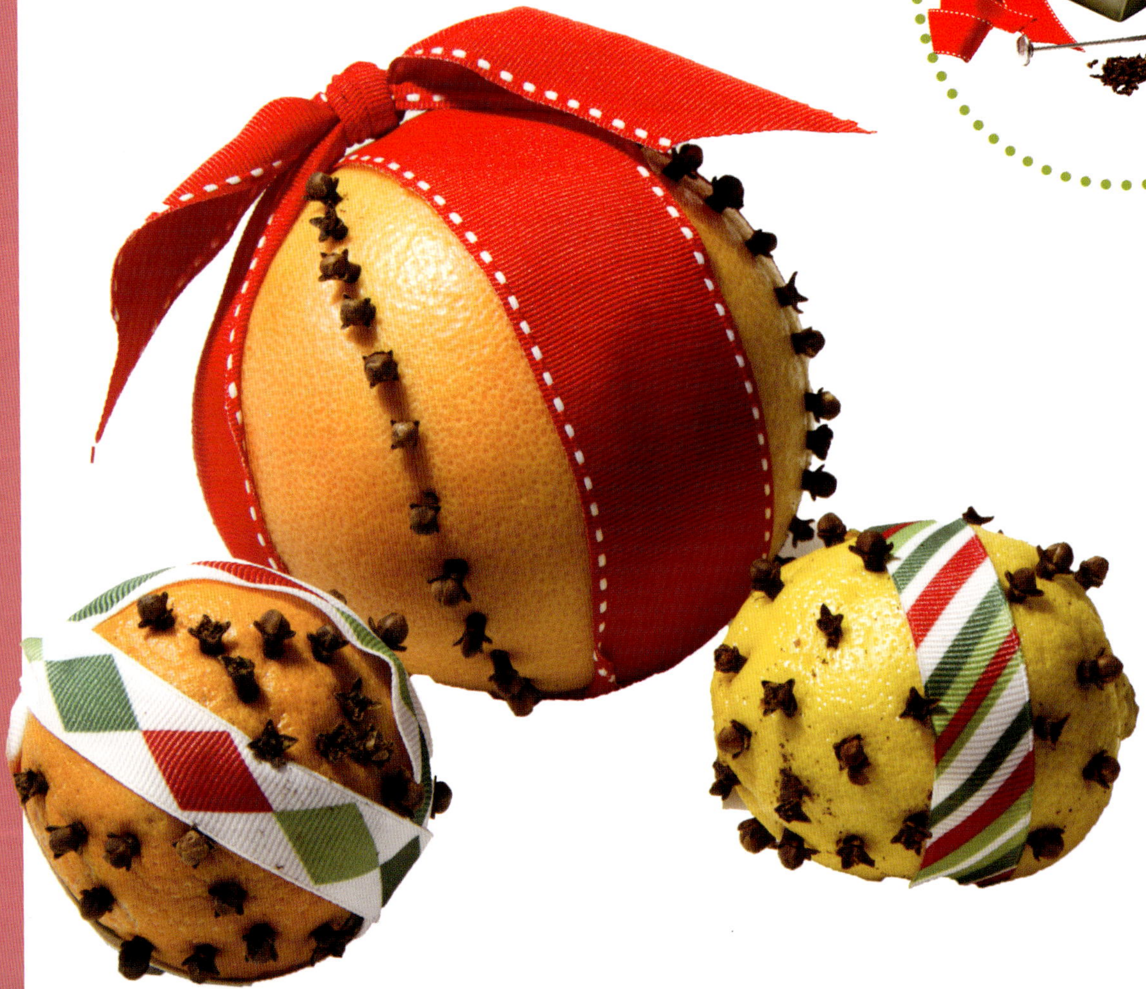

1 Wrap ribbon around an orange and secure with glue or pins for hanging.

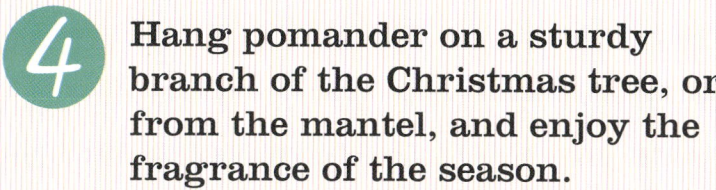

2 Use toothpicks, or meat thermometer, to punch holes in a pattern around the orange.

3 Fill in the holes with cloves.

4 Hang pomander on a sturdy branch of the Christmas tree, or from the mantel, and enjoy the fragrance of the season.

With just a few pieces of scrapbook paper you can create more than a dozen paper posies, super cute as a teacher gift, present for Grandma, or décor for your own home.

YOU WILL NEED

- Several pages of scrapbook paper
- Decorative-edge scissors or pinking shears
- Hole punch (small)
- Brads
- Assortment of coordinating embellishments (stickers, rub-ons, ribbon, etc.)
- Glue sticks
- Glue gun
- Chopsticks
- Foam block